HISTORY'S GREAT INVENTORS

PHILIP ARDAGH

ILLUSTRATED BY CHRIS MOULD

Belitha Press

First published in Great Britain in 1995 by
Belitha Press Limited
London House, Great Eastern Wharf,
Parkgate Road, London SW11 4NQ

Reprinted in 1996

ISBN 1 85561 585 1

Printed in Hong Kong

British Library Cataloguing in Publication Data
for this book is available from the
British Library.

Editor: Maria O'Neill
Designer: Hayley Cove
Consultant: Perry Williams

CONTENTS

INTRODUCTION

Every tool we use must have been invented by someone at some time. The origins of some inventions are lost in the mists of prehistory. For example, you won't find the names of the people who invented the wheel in here. But the achievements of later inventors are very well recorded.

Who is to say which inventors were great and which were not? Thomas Edison might be thought of as a great inventor for the sheer number of ideas he **patented**. People such as Marie Curie and James Martin could be called great because of the number of lives their inventions continue to save.

Some inventors are admired because their ideas are so clever. Others are considered great because of the simplicity of their solutions.

Between the covers of this book, you'll find some of the greatest and most inventive inventors in history.

Words in **bold** in the text are explained in the glossary on page 30.

ARCHIMEDES

Archimedes was what historians call an ancient Greek. That isn't to say that he lived to be ancient, though he did last into his mid-seventies. He would probably have survived even longer if he hadn't been killed by Roman soldiers. Born in the city of Syracuse on the island of Sicily in about 287 BC, Archimedes was, by birth, an enemy of Rome.

Archimedes is said to have invented many weapons for the armies of King Hieron of Syracuse to use against the invading Romans. There are tales of huge catapults, cranes with claw-like hooks to lift enemy ships straight out of the water, and even enormous mirrors.

According to legend, these mirrors were mounted on cliffs facing out to sea. When the Roman ships came into view, the mirrors were pointed towards the sun. The rays were then reflected on to the ships, causing them to burn and sink.

But Archimedes' most famous invention was the Archimedes screw. This was a giant wooden screw, cased in a wooden cylinder. The bottom end of the screw and cylinder was placed in water. When the screw was turned, it pulled the water up the sides of the cylinder and out of the top. This was used to bail water out of flooded ships, or even out of the ground.

Syracuse finally fell to the Romans in 212 BC and Archimedes was killed. The Roman general in charge, a man called Marcellus, was furious. He knew Archimedes was a great inventor and thinker and wanted his life spared.

Eureka!

The story goes that Archimedes worked out an important scientific principle while lying in a full bath. He realized that the amount of water slopping on to the floor was the same **volume** as his body, which was pushing it out of the bath. He was so excited that he leapt out shouting 'Eureka!', which means I have found it (the solution).

LEONARDO DA VINCI

Leonardo da Vinci was a great all-rounder. He was a brilliant painter, sculptor, architect, musician, **engineer** and scientist as well as one of history's greatest inventors. He was born in Vinci, in Italy, in 1452. His name is really a nickname meaning Leonardo of Vinci.

Leonardo studied under an artist called Andrea del Verrochio. According to one story, del Verrochio saw an angel that Leonardo had painted, and thought it was so much better than his own work that he gave up painting for life. Leonardo set up as an artist on his own in about 1477.

By 1482, Leonardo was – among other things – state engineer in Milan, and had invented an irrigation system to bring water to the plains of Lombardy. He was left handed and could write backwards in mirror writing. Leonardo also made sketches of his inventions. These included designs for various secret weapons, a type of hang glider, a submarine and a kind of helicopter. Most of these remarkable ideas remained just that, ideas on paper. All this from the man who also found time to paint the *Mona Lisa*, one of the most famous paintings in the world.

Discoveries from within

Leonardo was also interested in the inner workings of the human body. He made some incredibly detailed sketches of the human skeleton, organs, and nervous system. He even came close to realizing that blood is pumped around the body.

JOHANN GUTENBERG

Books have been with us for thousands of years but, until 500 years ago, every single one had to be written by hand. The German, Johann Gutenberg, born in about 1397, changed all this. He invented the first successful system of moveable type. Block printing came earlier but this was only good for short inscriptions, not whole books.

Moveable type is letters which are moved around to make up different words, and then moved again to make yet more words. These letters are cast in metal and can be used to print thousands of different books. Today, this method is taken for granted, but it took years of hard work for Gutenberg to perfect.

Block printing

Letters were carved into words, back-to-front, on a block of wood to make up a page of writing. Ink was rubbed on the block which was pressed on to paper – printing the words the right way around.

Gutenberg needed money to design and make his printing presses, but he didn't have any. At one stage he borrowed 800 guilders from a lawyer named Johann Fust. Later, they went into partnership. Gutenberg perfected his press and work began on printing the Bible in 1455.

Fust sprang into action. He was a smart businessman and saw the money-making opportunities the invention had to offer. He took Gutenberg to court and claimed that Gutenberg owed him 2000 guilders for the unpaid loan plus **interest**. Gutenberg couldn't pay, so Fust took over the press, printed 200 Bibles and kept the money from the sales. Gutenberg was ruined. He died penniless, but left his mark on the printed pages of history.

The Gutenberg Bible

The Bible that Gutenberg produced was the world's first printed Bible. It was 1282 pages long. Experts believe he needed 400 000 separate letters to print the whole book.

ALEXANDER GRAHAM BELL

Alexander Graham Bell was born in Scotland in 1847. His father, an expert on **elocution**, developed a way of teaching how words should be pronounced. This involved a written code of straight and curvy lines.

Bell became an elocution teacher and, when his mother went deaf, he became interested in the problems deaf people face. He decided to use his father's code to teach deaf children to speak.

In 1870, Bell and his family moved to Canada, in the hope that a warmer climate might improve their health. Bell travelled to Boston in the United States and started teaching deaf children. He used his knowledge of the human ear to invent a machine that could carry human speech along a wire. He built an electrical **transmitter** that vibrated like a person's eardrum.

The first telephone

Bell and Watson found a way for the transmitter of one telephone to turn speech into a varying electric current. The current travelled down a wire to the receiver of another telephone which vibrated on a disc and recreated the original speech.

Bell needed help with his experiments and asked a man named Thomas Watson to be his assistant.

On 10 March 1875, the world's first telephone call was made. Bell was in one room with his telephone at the ready. Watson sat in another room, the earpiece of his machine pressed eagerly against his ear. What memorable lines did Alexander Graham Bell utter on this momentous occasion?

Unfortunately, in the excitement, Bell knocked over the battery connected to the telephone. Some acid spilled from it on to his trousers. Leaping to his feet, the inventor cried: 'Mr Watson! Come here! I want you!' This was the rather uninspiring message of the world's first ever telephone call.

Within two years, the first telephone exchange had opened in Connecticut, USA.

Other inventions

In 1876, Bell invented the first electronic hearing aid. It was a clumsy device compared with modern aids, but a brilliant idea. He set up a laboratory that produced the first **phonographic record** – the forerunner of vinyl records, which were later replaced by CDs.

CHARLES BABBAGE

Charles Babbage was born in 1792, the son of a successful banker in the west of England. Babbage was a great inventor, but his two main inventions were never completed. His inventions paved the way for the modern computer age. Babbage was a highly intelligent person and was particularly interested in mathematics. He spotted mistakes in the published logarithm tables. These were tables of figures to make dividing and multiplying quicker and easier, in a time before mechanical or electronic calculators had been invented. The tables were very useful, but a few errors had crept in.

Babbage began work on building a machine which he called a 'difference engine'. He hoped that it would calculate logarithms automatically.
The British government liked the idea and funded his work. Each piece of the machine needed to move accurately for it to function properly. Unfortunately, there was one problem. The difference engine kept coming up with the wrong answers. After ten years, the funding stopped and the money ran out.

Babbage started work on a new invention, the 'analytical engine' which – he hoped – would be able to work out the hardest calculations.

Babbage spent 37 years working on the analytical engine, refining it and redesigning it. But the technology he needed for the machine to work properly had not yet been developed. He died frustrated, his dream unrealized.

The first computer programmer

Lady Ada Lovelace, daughter of Lord Byron the British Romantic poet, was the first computer programmer. She was an excellent mathematician and devised a number of programs for the analytical engine using special cards with holes punched in them. Lady Ada was a secret gambler and died in poverty.

Babbage's other great ideas

Babbage had earlier success with other ideas. These inventions included the cowcatcher, which was designed to sweep obstacles off railway tracks, and an ophthalmoscope for studying the back of the human eye.

MARY PHELPS JACOB

Mary Phelps Jacob is one of history's little known inventors. Her invention has been used by billions of people worldwide since 1914, but few people have ever heard of her. She married a millionaire called Harry Crosby and became Caresse Crosby – another name which means nothing to most people.

Mary Phelps Jacob was born into a well-to-do American family in 1892. She grew up at a time when women wore whalebone corsets under long dresses. A whalebone corset was a rigid undergarment worn laced up – as tightly as possible – at the back. It was designed to pull in the wearer's stomach and push up her bosom. The corsets were very uncomfortable, and some women fainted when wearing them too tight.

Mary Phelps Jacob became well-known in fashionable New York circles, often going to party after party, night after night. She became tired of trying to dance in her corset. In 1913, she had a brainwave. She designed the world's first brassiere, or bra. (The name comes from the French for bodice.) Her first bra, or **prototype**, was made from two handkerchiefs sewn together! She patented an improved version in 1914.

To begin with, this daring new invention caused shock and even outrage. But times were changing. Vast numbers of women now had the opportunity to go to work and people began to dress differently. Bras made it possible for women to wear practical blouses, skirts and suits instead of constricting, long dresses.

Mary Phelps Jacob lived until 1970, the start of the decade when some women stopped wearing their bras as a symbol of further freedom.

Brilliantly simple

It is easy to underestimate the brilliance of the bra because it seems such a simple idea. But an idea is only simple once someone has thought of it. It is the simplicity of Mary Phelps Jacob's invention that makes it truly great.

JAMES MARTIN

Irish engineer James Martin, born in 1893, originally set out to build lightweight aeroplanes and, following the outbreak of the Second World War, turned his attention to fighter planes. But James Martin is not remembered for an aircraft. His invention saved, and still saves, the lives of countless pilots. James Martin – later Sir James, but known to his friends as Sir Jimmy – invented the ejection seat.

Getting a pilot out of a fast-moving aircraft in an emergency was a very difficult problem to solve, from how the pilot left the plane to how he reached the ground safely. James Martin's ejection seat offered an ingenious solution.

The pilot pulls a handle which releases the canopy above the pilot's head – so that it blows away – and shoots the seat up through the opening. Once clear of the aircraft, a small parachute opens to slow down the seat, with the pilot still sitting in it. Then a second, larger, chute opens, pulling the pilot from the seat and carrying him gently back to earth.

Captain Valentine Baker

Martin-Baker, the company set up by James Martin and Valentine Baker, still makes ejection seats today. Valentine Baker was a test pilot. He was tragically killed when testing one of their planes in 1942.

Ejection seats very quickly became a standard feature of jet fighters and many other types of planes since the 1950s. In the first tests, volunteers were fired up ramps in seats rather than out of aircraft.

James Martin was injured when trying to stop a fight between two strangers near his home. They turned on him and cracked his skull. Doctors decided that they needed to replace the broken bone with a metal plate. The story goes that when James Martin saw the metal plate the hospital planned to use, he ordered the panel-beaters at his factory to make him a better one.

James Martin lived into his late eighties and regularly received messages of thanks from pilots whose lives his invention had saved.

Marie Curie

Marie Curie was one of the greatest scientists the world has ever known. She made some amazing discoveries, including the fact that some **cancerous tumours** can be destroyed with radiation. She invented **radiotherapy** as well as the term 'radiation' itself.

Marie Curie was born Marie Sklodovska in Poland in 1867, and married Pierre Curie, a French scientist, in 1895. Another French scientist, Henri Becquerel, discovered that a **mineral** called uranium gave off strange rays. These rays passed through most solid objects. Marie and Pierre decided to investigate this discovery further.

Uranium is found in an ore called pitchblende. Marie and Pierre found that pitchblende gave off even more rays, or radiation, than uranium. They worked out that it contains more radioactive elements. After many years, the Curies discovered two new elements. They called the first one polonium after Poland, and the second radium, which is Latin for ray. In 1903, Pierre and Marie were awarded the **Nobel prize** for physics.

For the good of humankind

Marie Curie never patented any of her ideas. If she had, she would have died a very rich woman. She believed that her work – and the good that might come from it – belonged, not to her, but to humankind.

Three years later, in Paris, Pierre stepped into the road and was knocked down by an on-coming milk cart. He was killed. Marie carried on their work and faced dangers of her own. She worked in a draughty shed without protection from the harmful radiation.

In 1911, Marie won the Nobel prize again – this time for chemistry. Then, in Paris in 1914, the Institute of Radium was set up to study radiation and radiotherapy. Marie Curie held a senior post, and worked there with her elder daughter Irène.

Marie Curie died in 1934, as a result of her constant exposure to radiation. Her discoveries, which give hope and life to thousands of cancer sufferers, had finally killed her.

WERNHER VON BRAUN

On 20 July 1969, American astronaut Neil Armstrong became the first person to set foot on the moon. His name will never be forgotten, but who made it all possible? An inventor called Wernher von Braun.

Born in Germany in 1912, the son of a wealthy baron, von Braun studied to be an engineer in Berlin. As a student he became interested in space travel and promised himself that one day he would send a rocket to the moon.

Von Braun and some of his fellow students rented a warehouse in Kummersdorf near Berlin. They built their own small rockets and launched them in a nearby field. They raised money by charging people to watch.

In June 1935, some German army officers came to one of the launches and von Braun ended up as chief of an experimental rocket station. But the German army wasn't interested in trips to the moon. They realized that a rocket could be a useful weapon.

Arrested by Nazis

During the war, von Braun was put in prison by the **Nazis**. They knew that he wasn't happy designing weapons, and thought he might try to flee to Britain. But the German army needed him so he was soon released and sent back to work.

When the Second World War broke out, von Braun and a team of engineers were ordered to design rocket bombs. The result was the V2 rockets fired from Germany across the Channel. V2s regularly landed and exploded in Britain, killing hundreds of people.

In 1945, von Braun and some of his team gave themselves up to the United States army. The war was over, but he was still making military rockets, this time in America for the Americans. All this changed in 1957, the year the **Soviet Union** launched *Sputnik 1*, the first space satellite.

The race to the moon began, with Wernher von Braun as the director of a new space centre in Houston, Texas. At last his dream came true. He and his team built a rocket to fly to the moon.

Apollo 11

Apollo 11 was the rocket that took Neil Armstrong, 'Buzz' Aldrin and Michael Collins to the moon and back. The landing unit was called *Eagle*. Armstrong and Aldrin took *Eagle* to the moon while Collins orbited in the rocket's command module.

Maria the Jewess

Maria the Jewess wrote under the name Miriam, sister of Moses. If you think that's strange, wait until you hear a few of her scientific theories.

Maria lived in the first century AD in Alexandria, Egypt. Science in those days was mainly carried out by **alchemists**. These were people who put their efforts into trying to turn base metals into gold. Their craft was a mixture of hocus-pocus, trickery and basic science.

Maria believed that certain types of metal were male and others were female. Her theory was that if a male and female metal were united – perhaps melted and mixed together – they might produce an offspring that was a third, different type of metal.

Although the male-female idea sounds funny today, she was on the right track. When some different metal **elements** are joined to create a compound, the new metal compound is very different from the metals that went together to create it.

Maria the Jewess was also a successful inventor. She designed some scientific apparatus that was still being used until surprisingly recently. The most famous of her inventions is probably the bain-marie, which was named after her. This is a special kind of water boiler designed to keep the substances in it at the same, steady temperature at all times.

Although Maria the Jewess made no startling scientific discoveries, her inventions helped scientists of later eras make discoveries of their own.

Thomas Edison

Thomas Edison was born in Ohio in America in 1847. He was brilliant at spotting the potential of other people's inventions, and at making the best use of them. He spent much of his later life in huge legal battles, trying to stop other people copying the inventions he had patented. By the time he died in 1931, Edison had patented more than 1093 inventions, many of them involving electricity.

Edison developed an interest in electricity while working in a **telegraph** office. He was given the job after saving a telegraph agent's son from the path of an approaching train. In 1878, an Englishman called Joseph Swan invented the first electric light bulb after working on it for 20 years. A year later, Edison came up with his own version.

Although Swan had been first, Edison was quick to accuse him of stealing the idea. They were soon hurling abuse at each other across the Atlantic.

Edison's light bulb

Inside the glass bulb was a carbon **filament** in a partial vacuum. The filament glowed when it was heated by an electric current, giving off electric light.

Edison improved his light bulb and eventually the two men joined forces to form the Edison and Swan Electric Company.

Electric light changed the world. People no longer needed to light candles, oil lamps or gas lamps. Electricity now lit up a room at the flick of a switch. It was clean, safe and convenient.

Of course, for a light bulb to work in a house, the electricity had to be **generated** and a power supply connected. Edison worked at this and, in September 1881, the world's first electricity power station opened in Pearl Street, New York.

The dream team

In 1876, Edison set up a laboratory and workshop in Menlo Park, near New York. His team dreamed up lamps, vacuum pumps, electricity generators, early movie equipment, phonographs and even talking dolls. Edison was famous for working day and night without a rest!

OTHER GREAT INVENTORS

Galileo Galilei
(1564 – 1642)

Italian astronomer, scientist and inventor who made an improved version of the **telescope** (the first telescope was invented a year earlier by the Dutchman Hans Lippershey). Galileo also came up with the idea for the **pendulum clock** and made many new discoveries in astronomy.

Joseph Lister (1827 – 1912)

Lister was the Englishman who improved a patient's chance of survival after an operation. He invented methods of getting rid of the germs which cause a wound to become infected during surgery in hospitals.

George Stephenson
(1781 – 1848)

In 1825, George Stephenson completed the world's first public railway. The first passenger train was pulled by his locomotive, the *Locomotion*. His most famous locomotive was *The Rocket*, built with his son Robert. In 1829, it won a competition for the best locomotive, travelling at a staggering 48 km per hour.

Wilbur (1867 – 1912) and Orville (1871 – 1948) Wright

The Wright brothers invented the first real aeroplane. In 1903, Orville piloted their plane, the *Flyer* in the first powered, controlled flight. It was such a remarkable achievement that few people believed them. But soon they were world famous.

Frank Whittle
(1907 –   )

Englishman Frank Whittle invented the jet engine, which he patented in 1930. The first aeroplane powered by a Whittle jet engine took off in 1941. Whittle's invention changed the way we travel forever.

Gottlieb Daimler
(1834 – 1900)

Daimler was the German who invented the first petrol-powered car in 1886. Another German, Karl Benz, invented the first proper motorcar, but Daimler's car became the prototype for the cars on today's roads.

GLOSSARY

alchemists: people who lived hundreds of years ago and carried out experiments that were a mixture of chemistry and hocus-pocus.

cancerous tumours: growths inside people, or animals, caused by cells in the body dividing abnormally.

elements: any of more than 100 substances that cannot be broken down or separated by ordinary chemical means. Gold and carbon are examples of elements.

elocution: the art of speaking clearly.

engineer: a person who applies scientific methods to the design and construction of machines, roads and buildings.

filament: the wire inside an electric light bulb that gives off light when heated by an electric current.

generated: made or produced. In this case, electricity produced in a power station.

interest: a charge for lending money.

mineral: a solid substance which is not living, such as rock.

Nazis: members of Adolf Hitler's fascist party in Germany.

Nobel prize: prizes awarded for outstanding achievement in areas from science to peace. The prizes are named after Alfred Nobel, the Swedish inventor of dynamite, who left money for the awards.

patented: something which has a patent. A patent is a legal permit which prevents everyone except the person who has taken out the patent (often the inventor) from making or selling the invention. People patent inventions so that others cannot steal their ideas.

pendulum clock: a clock with a free-swinging pendulum beneath it.

phonographic record: an early form of recording sounds, originally on a wax cylinder. It was replaced by the vinyl record, which was replaced by the CD.

prototype: the first version, or one of the first versions, of an invention. The prototype can be tested and improved if necessary.

radiotherapy: the treatment of cancer with controlled doses of radiation.

Soviet Union: an area from eastern Europe to central and northern Asia that was ruled by communism. Established in 1922, it was controlled from Russia but was disbanded in 1991.

telegraph: a system of sending and receiving messages along wires with electricity.

telescope: an instrument which magnifies distant objects. Astronomers use telescopes to study the stars.

transmitter: a device which sends out sound waves or radio waves.

volume: the amount of space inside or taken up by an object.

WHEN THEY LIVED

c 287 – 212 BC	Archimedes
c 100 AD	Maria the Jewess
c 1397 – 1468	Johann Gutenberg
1452 – 1519	Leonardo da Vinci
1564 – 1642	Galileo Galilei
1781 – 1848	George Stephenson
1792 – 1871	Charles Babbage
1827 – 1912	Joseph Lister
1834 – 1900	Gottlieb Daimler
1847 – 1931	Thomas Edison
1847 – 1922	Alexander Graham Bell
1867 – 1934	Marie Curie
1867 – 1948	The Wright brothers
1892 – 1970	Mary Phelps Jacob
1893 – 1981	James Martin
1907 –	Frank Whittle
1912 – 1977	Wernher von Braun

INDEX